A First Book of
VERDI

FOR THE BEGINNING PIANIST with DOWNLOADABLE MP3s

David Dutkanicz

Dover Publications, Inc.
Mineola, New York

All music available as downloadable MP3s

Go to www.doverpublications.com/048683896X
to access these files.

Bibliographical Note

A First Book of Verdi: For the Beginning Pianist with Downloadable MP3s is a new work,
first published by Dover Publications, Inc., in 2019.

International Standard Book Numbers
ISBN-13: 978-0-486-83896-0
ISBN-10: 0-486-83896-X

Manufactured in the United States by LSC Communications
83896X01
www.doverpublications.com

2 4 6 8 10 9 7 5 3 1

2019

Contents

Introduction

Let us turn to the past—
that will be progress.

—Giuseppe Verdi

A First Book of Verdi continues the Dover tradition of making the music of the masters accessible to all. Giuseppe Verdi (1813–1901) is revered today as a master of opera, having elevated the form to new levels. He composed over twenty-five of them and a number of memorable vocal works as well. As you play the pieces throughout this book, you will recognize themes that have become part of the musical canon. Verdi was celebrated during his life and remains one of the most performed composers to this day.

The selections presented here were carefully selected to represent his style and arranged to be more accessible. Fingerings are provided as suggestions and should be customized for each individual. Phrasing and pedaling are recommended minimally so as to make the music less daunting, and the compositions can be filled in as progress is made. The melodic and technical insight of these excerpts can serve as a tool for developing technique and, more importantly, as a means to discover the richness and depth found in the vast music of Verdi.

"Anvil Chorus"
from *Il Trovatore*

This famous melody is from the opera *Il Trovatore* ("The Troubadour"), which premiered in 1853. It tells the story of a Spanish count hopelessly in love, and the jealousy and intrigue that follow. In this scene, a chorus of Gypsies sings: "So to work now / Lift up your hammers!"

Allegro moderato

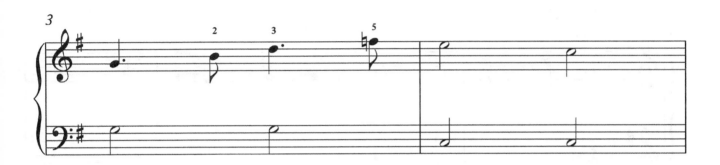

"Now to Die"

from *Ernani*

Ernani is not as well known as Verdi's other works, but it was a huge success after its premiere and became a staple of many opera companies. The plot revolves around the outlawed nobleman Don Juan of Aragon, who has become the bandit Ernani. He is distraught over his one true love forcibly marrying another and tragically tries to rescue her. In this scene, Ernani and his love, Elvira, have met after a long absence and ponder how content they are together.

Andantino

Prelude

from *Il Trovatore*

This excerpt from the prelude of *Il Trovatore* presents a lovely theme that recurs throughout the opera. When practicing, notice that many passages in the right hand use the same fingerings (e.g., measures 5–6 and 7–8). It is helpful to memorize these fingerings, which allows you to focus more energy on the performance.

"Come in quest'ora bruna"

from *Simon Boccanegra*

The title of this aria translates to "As in This Dark Hour" and is sung by Maria, under the name of Amelia. As she looks out to the sea and remembers an old woman who raised her, she promises never to forget her humble background. There are some wide leaps in the right-hand melody (e.g., measures 3 and 9). Be sure to practice these separately, so they are played smoothly.

Cantabile

"Heavenly Aida"

from *Aida*

Aida centers around a slave girl living in Egypt. This charming aria is sung by Radamès, a soldier in love with her. Play gently, and review the accidentals in the last nine measures before practicing. The sharps are meant to add a celestial feel to the music as Radamès sings: "Heavenly Aida, divine form / Mystical garland of light and flowers / You are queen of my thoughts / You are the splendor of my life."

"Chorus of the Hebrew Slaves"

from *Nabucco*

Nabucco is based on the biblical books of Jeremiah and Daniel and is set during the Babylonian captivity of Israel. This chorus has become increasingly popular over the years, turning into an anthem for many different people and their causes. It also is known by its original title *"Va, pensiero"* ("Hasten, Thoughts").

Andante

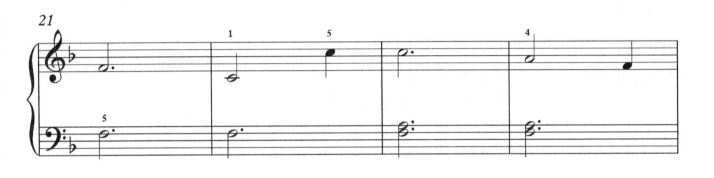

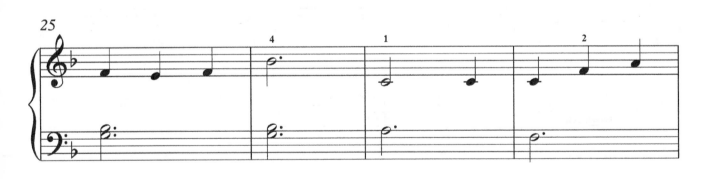

Overture

from *Macbeth*

Operas typically begin with an overture, which serves as an introduction to the musical themes of the story and occasionally foreshadows some of the action. This overture opens *Macbeth,* which used an Italian libretto based on Shakespeare's famous play. Note the contrast created by the dynamics, and use them to make your playing more musical.

Moderato

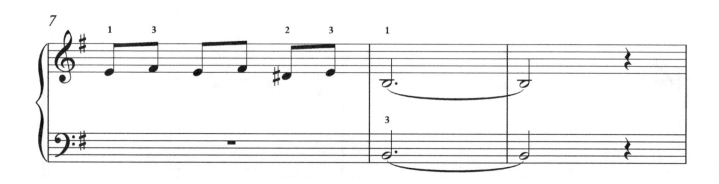

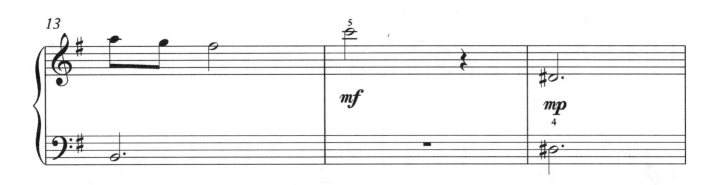

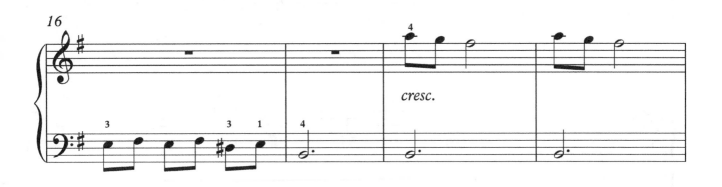

Prelude

from *Jerusalem*

Jerusalem is an opera set in France and Palestine just before the time of the First Crusade (circa 1100 CE). This excerpt contains a very dramatic effect in its opening. Note the instruction *crescendo poco a poco sempre* ("become louder gradually and continually"). At measure 1, begin softly and become increasingly louder until reaching the *forte* of measure 7.

Prelude to Act III

from *La Traviata*

La Traviata is one of Verdi's most famous works, frequently performed to this day. It premiered in 1853 and received a tepid response, mostly due to a poor performance. However, within a year, the opera was recast and the new production was a hit, propelling the work to the top of the repertory.

"Dio, che nell'alma infondere amor"

from *Don Carlos*

This famous duet, which translates to "O God, Who Fills Our Hearts with Love," is sung between the title character, Don Carlos, and his close friend Rodrigo. Once the two are reunited after a long absence, they pledge their loyalty to each other with this song. Play warmly, and note the effect created when the melody is played a third apart.

Moderato

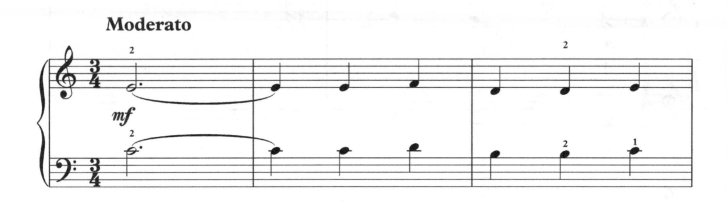

(Turn page.)

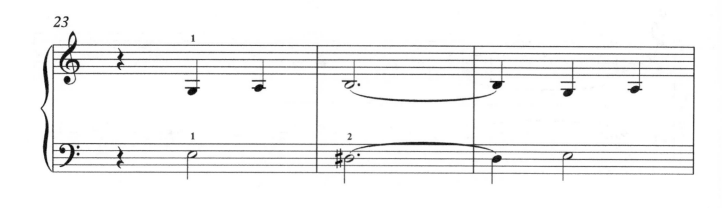

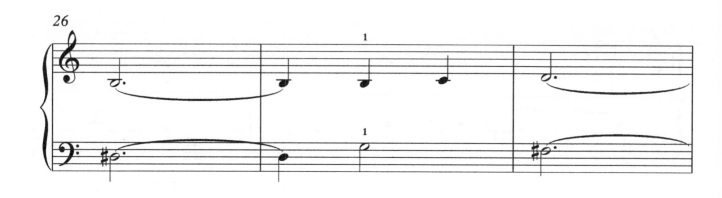

"Ah, la paterna mano"
from *Macbeth*

This moving aria is from the final act of *Macbeth* and translates to "The Hands of the Father." The text reads: "Ah, the hands of the father did not defend you my dear ones, from the hired brutes that wounded you unto death." Note Verdi's use of chromaticism here. Although the key is C major, all Es are flat to create a sense of C minor without changing keys.

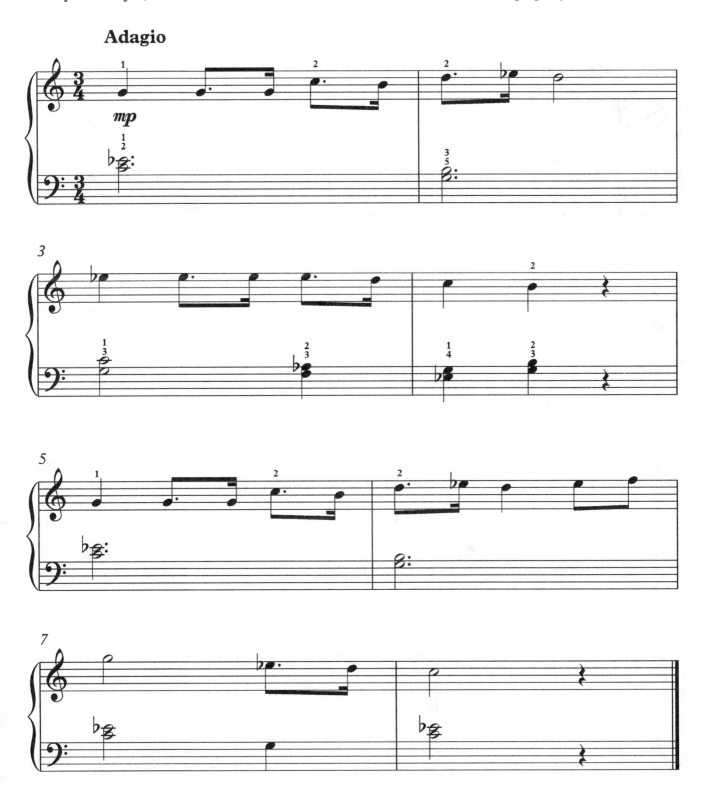

Act III, Scene 2 (opening)

from *Falstaff*

Falstaff is a comic work and Verdi's final opera. It is based on Shakespeare's *The Merry Wives of Windsor* and *Henry IV, Parts 1 and 2,* and tells the story of Sir John Falstaff, a "fat and old" knight who has his sights set on two rich women to fix his financial woes. Despite initial success, the opera fell into obscurity and was only revived in the twentieth century by the conductor Arturo Toscanini.

Requiem

(opening)

Verdi's setting of the Catholic Mass for the Dead (requiem) is one of the most powerful music works and is considered an "opera in disguise." Play the opening in a soft tone, and note the accidentals toward the end of the piece before playing.

Sinfonia

from *Nabucco*

This *sinfonia* (symphony) serves a similar role as an overture. It opens a new act or scene and introduces themes of the characters. Play in a majestic manner, fit for a king. *Nabucco* is Italian for "Nebuchadnezzar," who was ruler of the Babylonian Empire during the time the opera is set.

Maestoso

"Adio, mio cor, mia vita"

from *Jerusalem*

This is sung as a duet in the opera *Jerusalem*, and the title of this touching work translates to "Goodbye, My Heart, My Life." Play with a melancholy tone and at a walking pace (*andantino*). Pay close attention to the left hand in measure 6: the E-flat and F will sound dissonant at first but will resolve by half step respectively to D and G on the next beat.

Andantino

"Laudi"

from *Four Sacred Pieces*

This collection of four sacred works, originally entitled *Quattro pezzi sacri*, includes an Ave Maria, Stabat Mater, and Te Deum. This work (full title "Laudi alla Vergine Maria") is based on a short prayer found in Dante's "Paradiso." Play with a reverent tone, emulating the original unaccompanied chorus.

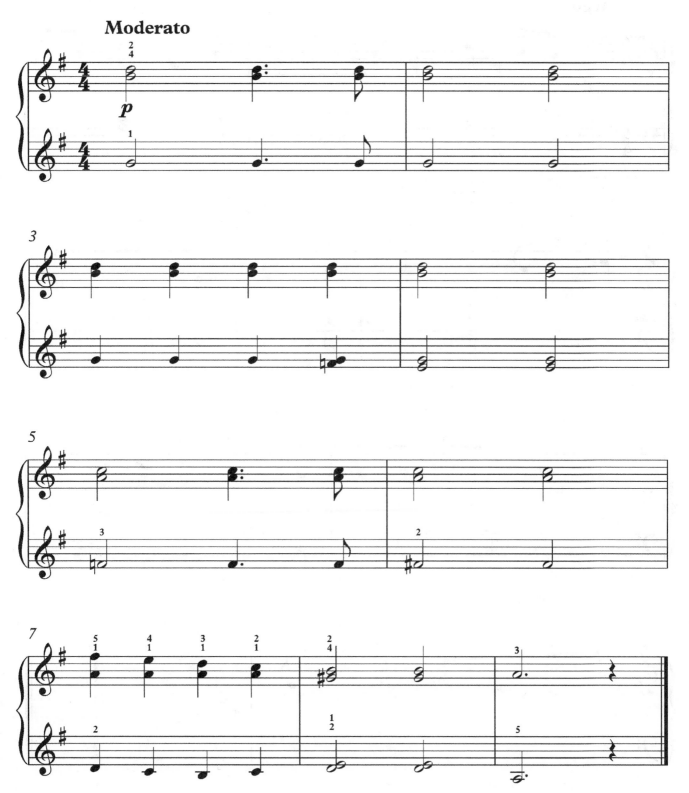

Lacrymosa

from *Requiem*

Lacrymosa (Latin for "weeping") is a movement within the Dies Irae of the requiem. Note the tempo (*largo*), and play this selection slowly and with expression. Add pedal as needed to sustain the tone and mood of the music.

Gran Scena

from *Macbeth*

In opera, a *gran scena* involves an extended passage of monologue (or dialogue) where the narrative of the story is revealed. In this excerpt, the story is told at an *adagio* tempo. Keep the tempo slow, but do not drag the music. Propel the melody forward using expression, and be sure to play the triplets in measure 7 evenly between both hands.

"Ave Maria"

from *Otello*

In this scene, Desdemona, Othello's wife, kneels in prayer for all those who are suffering as she is. The opening is reminiscent of a Gregorian chant as she recites the "Ave Maria." In the second section, Desdemona says a personal prayer. Review the accidentals before practicing, and use them to increase the emotion of the music.

Slowly

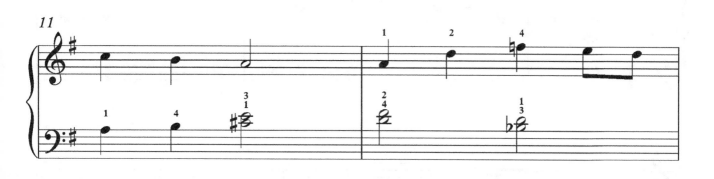

"Bella figlia dell'amore"

from *Rigoletto*

This memorable excerpt from *Rigoletto* translates to "Beautiful Daughter of Love." In the opera, it is sung as a quartet between Rigoletto, his daughter Gilda, the Duke, and Maddalena, the Duke's latest romantic interest. Play in an even manner, being careful not to rush or drag the sixteenth notes.

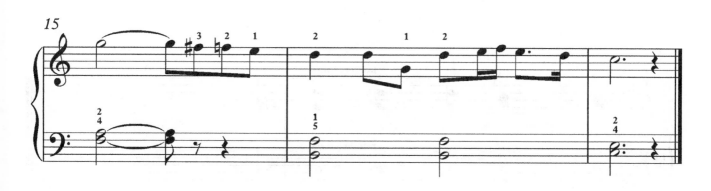

"La vergine degli angeli"

from *La Forza del Destino*

La Forza del Destino ("The Force of Destiny") is set in Spain and involves the tragic love story of Leonara, the Marquis's daughter, and Don Alvaro, a soldier from South America, who cannot wed because of his station in life. The title means "Virgin of the Angels" and is performed during a church scene. Play in a somber mode, keeping the rhythms equal in both hands.

Adagio

"Romanza"

from *Un Ballo in Maschera*

The title of this opera means "A Masked Ball," and the story revolves around the assassination of King Gustav III of Sweden, who was shot while attending a masquerade. Verdi had a frustrating time with the censors of the day, who eventually forced him to change the setting to colonial Boston. Nonetheless, the music remained untouched and it became a beloved opera staple.

Andante

"Grand March"
from *Aida*

Accompanied by a stage full of soldiers, officers, bound prisoners, and an elephant or two, this march announces the victorious return of Egypt's army. This is one of opera's most memorable moments and one of Verdi's most celebrated works. Imagine this wild and majestic scene, and play with all the appropriate pomp and vigor you can muster.

Maestoso

"Drinking Song"
from *La Traviata*

This famous melody is part of an Italian tradition known as a *brindisi* ("toast"). In this scene of revelry, the chorus sings: *"Libiamo ne' lieti calici"* ("Let us drink from the joyful chalices"). Play with a lively tempo and joyful character.

Moderato

Sinfonia

from *Oberto*

Oberto is Verdi's first opera, which paved the way for his future career. It premiered at Milan's famous La Scala Opera, and its moderate success led to new commissions, one of which was the breakthrough opera *Nabucco*. Note in this excerpt how the first eight measures serve as a dramatic introduction, while the last eight measures introduce the theme.

Andante mosso

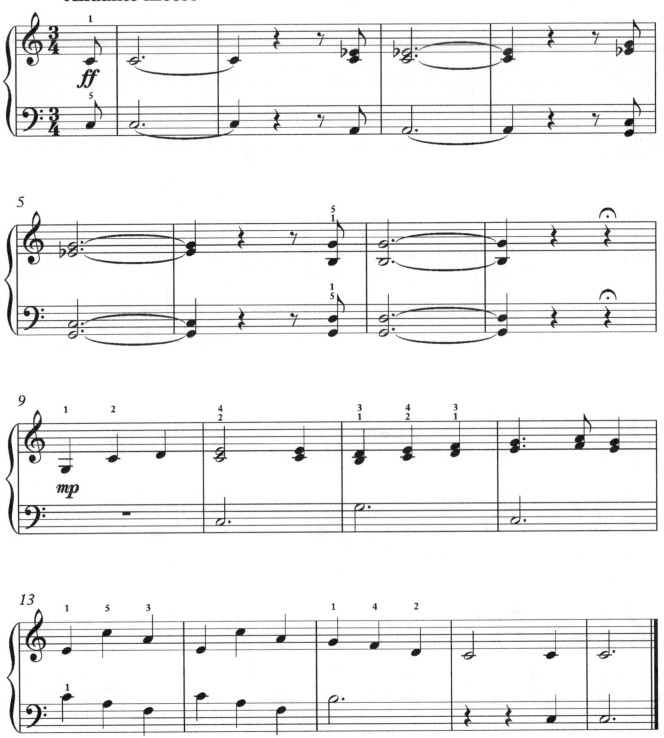

Overture

from *Luisa Miller*

This tragic opera is based on Friedrich Schiller's play *Love and Intrigue*. Miller is a retired soldier looking after his daughter, Luisa, who is in love with a suspicious stranger. The tragic bond between father and daughter deepens as the identity of the stranger is revealed and more characters are involved. Play this excerpt expressively, using the left-hand pattern to accent the tone of the scene.

Moderato

Prelude to Act III

from *Un Ballo in Maschera*

In the opening of this opera's final scene, a murder is plotted as invitations to the masked ball arrive. Be sure to practice the left hand separately, playing the notes evenly in rhythm and in tone. The right-hand melody should be lyrical and not overpowered by the accompaniment. Be mindful of the *ritardando* in measures 7 and 16. Use the changes in tempo to add expression to the music.

Sweetly

Sinfonia

from *Aroldo*

Aroldo tells the tale of a crusading knight in the Middle Ages and is set in Kent and Loch Lomond. The *sinfonia* opens the work and is similar to a chorale, setting the tone for the story. There are three voices, and each should be played equally.

Andante

Duet

from *Il Trovatore*

In this scene, Manrico, a troubadour and officer in the Prince's army, sings a duet with Azucena, a Gypsy woman who may be Manrico's mother. A melodic technique known as "octave displacement" appears in measures 12–13. Rather than moving one step from E–F, Verdi moves the F up an octave for dramatic effect.

Andantino

Sinfonia

from *Les Vêpres Siciliennes*

Les Vêpres Siciliennes ("The Sicilian Vespers") is one of Verdi's more political operas. The title is derived from a successful rebellion of Sicily against French occupiers in the thirteenth century and reflected the national aspirations of Italy at the time. The tragic story mirrors *Romeo and Juliet*, as two lovers fall victim to their fighting families. Carefully review the accidentals, and pay attention to how the chromatic notes heighten the tension of the story.

Act III (opening)

from *La Forza del Destino*

Verdi opens the third act of this opera with a consistent pattern of eight notes in the accompaniment. This is designed to create a pulse that complements the melody and breathes some energy after the previous section. Review the left-hand fingerings, and customize them to create as little repositioning of the wrist as possible. This will help ease practice and performance of the work.

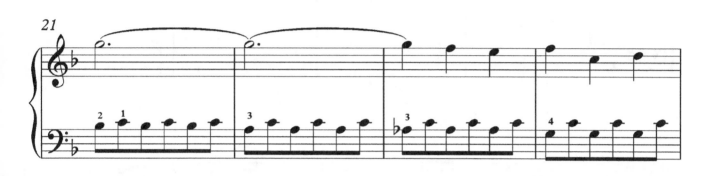

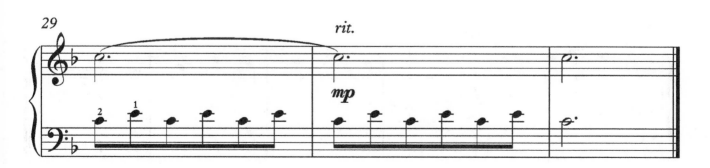

"La donna è mobile"

from *Rigoletto*

This popular aria is sung by the Duke in the beginning of Act III. The title translates to "The Woman Is Fickle," with the inherent irony being that the Duke himself is the ficklest character in the story. Many famous tenors, from Enrico Caruso to Luciano Pavarotti, have recorded this work. Perform in a playful manner and with a light character.